Wal
arour

By Damien Enright

Georgian country house, Brown's Mills, Kinsale

A Merlin Press Publication

Published by Merlin Press 1998

ISBN 1 902631 01 3

Design by Sean O'Leary
Photos by John Collins and Naomi Yamaguchi
Illustrations by Dan O' Connell

MERLIN PRESS
The Old Courthouse, Timoleague, Co. Cork
Tel; +353 (0)23 46493 Fax: +353 (0)23 46045
Email: prolang@tinet.ie

Contents

Five easy, circular walks in West Cork's lovely scenery and clean air. Average distance from Cork, 18 miles, Bandon, 9, Clonakilty, 14.

Dedicated to

my patient wife, children, friends and dog,
who have made life's roads a pleasure
and lightened my steps on the way.

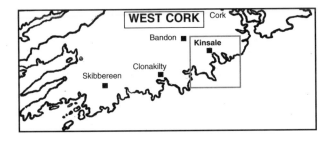

There is no guarantee that a walk outlined in this book is a right-of-way.
The author and supporters of this book do not accept any responsibility for
trespass nor for accident or loss to or by the public in walking these routes.

This publication has been supported by
the West Cork LEADER Co-operative

A note on walking

The Irish are big on walking. If there is one thing we have plenty of, it is back roads and fresh air.

There are the power walkers, the Walking Women of Ireland, plugging along country roads with hips and shoulders swinging, out for the exercise after an already much-exercised day. The glow of their cheeks and the litheness of their stride attests the beneficial effects of 'exercise walking'.

Irish men, on the other hand, seem oblivious to walking's cosmetic effect, an unfortunate oversight on their part. Males are not seen striding along country lanes. When we do see a male abroad, he is generally being pulled along at a heart-stopping pace by two fist-fulls of dog leads, his greyhounds taking him for a run, rather than the other way around. Other encounters will involve men in caps, with fags in mouth and pockets full of fivers, out following the road bowling, after which they will walk miles.

There are the hill walkers and long-distance route marchers, doughty folk in serious boots, with ashplants, maps and small rucksacks. To them, we owe the opening up of green roads and byways, and the mapping of mountain trails not trodden since the ancient Celts made their way across country via uplands, the plains being covered with a dense growth of trees.

I, myself, do not power walk, greyhound follow, or road bowl wager. I walk for the curiosity and the uplift, the wonderments of the wayside and the 'high' of the free-flowing endorphins released after twenty minutes on the hoof. I am not so much a slow walker as one who is waylaid by the roadside attractions. Curiosity, atmosphere or amazement delays me, and while the company forges ahead, I am left behind, in thrall.

The walks outlined in this book are for walkers such as I. They take, generally, just a couple of hours but can easily be stretched to fill half a day. They are perfect for a weekend afternoon or a holiday meander.

They will, hopefully, stimulate my perambulating neighbours towards new horizons and inform visitors of the lovely land that awaits just off the tourist trail. I cannot imagine these local by-ways ever becoming crowded. We may in time meet a party of ardent Japanese, led by a person with a flag, or stout Austrians in lederhosen and braces singing "Falderee-Falderah". They will be sure of a welcome. We Irish delight in showing off our land.

To the farmers and landowners

But for the goodwill of farmers and landowners our enjoyment of Ireland's lovely landscape would be curtailed. Most of the walks here outlined are on lanes and back roads but roads do not always conveniently join up. To make circular routes - where one does not have to return home by the way one came - I have sometimes found old tracks, not often used. I have spoken personally to the landowners and farmers whose ground is crossed. They have not only been cooperative, but wish well to the walker. They reasonably point out, however, that walkers crossing their property must accept that they do so at their own risk.

I would like, particularly, to thank and give credit to Jerome Desmond and to Dick and Marion O'Sullivan, whose land is crossed on the Tisaxon Walk. In putting no let or hindrance on walkers, they demonstrate that the Irish tradition of courtesy and welcome to strangers is still alive.

The area

Kinsale is quite a surprise, even for a native Irishman. Quite unlike the generally flat, higgledy-piggledy conurbations with which we are familiar, it rises up from the sea in terraces, it is organised in rows. The 'cowboy' towns of West Cork have their robust charm, but Kinsale has a quaint organisation which, amazingly, has survived. The past is evident at every corner, the shadows and echoes are in every street. Ascending from the harbour in narrow lane ways with weather-slated houses and steeples like Normandy, it is unlike anywhere else on the Irish island.

Many native towns have preserved isolated historic buildings; Kinsale, perhaps uniquely, has preserved almost the entire historic town. Kinsale people have long had a talent for self preservation whether in dealing with the Spanish, Cromwell, or the English crown. Despite a battering from the guns of Mountjoy and of William of Orange, even the architecture has survived well.

Kinsale is a big town. Its size, discovered when one roams the hidden lanes high over the harbour, is another surprise. It has a waterfront, with promenades, two piers and three marinas. Boats and sailing has always been a motif. Visiting Kinsale one day in the mid 1940's - when the town was a backwater with derelict warehouses where there are now pied-a-terres - my father took up sympathetic conversation with a sun-browned, wind-burned, underweight refugee family in a ramshackle sailing barge tied to the dock. Stateless people, he told me later, fleeing war torn Europe, their home a leaky boat. I can remember them, and old Kinsale behind them, to this day.

It was then, indeed, a different place, long forgotten and not yet rediscovered. There it lay, mouldering in past glories, shop windows shuttered, slates missing, doors nailed up. Who could have imagined it as the resort it is now, gourmet restaurants abounding, sailing clubs and golf courses, restored buildings and refurbished streets? Kinsale is a triumph of community survival, of community effort, of a community finding pride in itself.

To walk around Kinsale - and there is no other way the town can be fully enjoyed - is to be overwhelmed by views, and haunted by history. The environs are equally seductive. While the town is sophisticated and cosmopolitan, the countryside around is natural and Irish. You are as likely to see an otter, a kingfisher or a bog iris outside Kinsale as anywhere else in West Cork. While the local coast and countryside has more than its share of monuments - forts, ruined castles, mills and churches - it has the clean sea, the big river, the verdant bohreens and the burgeoning flora and fauna of the mild Gulf Stream coast.

Within the town, history; outside it, history with natural history, besides. Kinsale has great and diverse walking. The effort of perambulation upon two feet is, alone, required for its enjoyment, but the exercise is short, sweet, and well worthwhile.

SOURCES
Mr John Thuillier's field study, "History of Kinsale", has been an invaluable source of information in the compilation of this book.

Walk No.1: Town and Country. 2 hours – about 2.5 miles.

Town and Country.

Town centre - Kinsale waterfront and harbour - the Bandon estuary - Commoge Marsh and Wildlife Sanctuary - the historic Old Town of Kinsale.

Locality: OS Map Sheet 87 Squares 6349, 6450, 6250, 6350 Kinsale town and west. The walk begins and ends at the town centre.

Description and Distance: A loop walk of 2.5 miles

Walking Time: 2 hours

Walking conditions: Pavements and quiet roads. A gentle climb for a quarter of a mile. Town streets.

Features: An excursion beyond the town. First, the waterside, with boats, yachts and fishing boats. Then, the broad Bandon River and Commoge Marsh where, through three seasons - early summer excepted - most of Ireland's water bird species can be readily viewed. Non-migrant juveniles of some species are still present in summer. From Commoge, our route climbs gently to panoramic views of the harbour, and then returns, via historic streets and buildings, to the starting point.

Flora and fauna: Water birds are the principal fauna on this walk. Of the ducks, teal, widgeon, mallard, shelduck and, occasionally, merganser are seen. The waders include godwits, redshank and greenshank, curlew, lapwing, dunlin, golden plover and ring plover. Cormorants are common; great northern divers are sometimes present in the harbour. Kestrels, grey crows and ravens are the main predators. Localised birds are stonechats and linnets. Spring migrants follow the Bandon River inland.

Equipment: Comfortable shoes are quite adequate for this walk, all on pavements or tarred by-roads.

Itinerary

(1) Starting outside the Tourist Office in Kinsale, we walk to the left, along the waterfront, past the marinas, towards the pier. One sees across the mud flats or water of the Inner Harbour - depending on the tide - the salient of Scilly, with its imposing old buildings on the shore. The name may come from 'sally' osiers which

Bandon River and foreshore

grew there, and were woven for lobster pots. Or, more fancifully, some Scilly Islander pirates may have made a haven there long ago.

The Pier Road, along which we walk, was built in the last century. Before then, the area to our right - the town park and gardens in front of Acton's Hotel - was under water, with knuckles of quays protruding into the harbour at right angles. In 1703, Alexander Selkirk, the Scottish sailor whose solitary sojourn on a 'desert' island inspired Defoe's "Robinson Crusoe", shipped out from Kinsale. In the 17th century, and again in the 19th, Kinsale was an important fishing port. Local historians refer to the report of the Irish Fishery Office, 1829, which records almost 7,000 persons engaged in catching or processing fish, building boats or servicing the industry.

For the spring mackerel season, large fleets of boats from Cornwall and the Isle of Man assembled, and fish, salted or packed in ice brought from Norway, was shipped to the English markets.

To exploit the development of a second mackerel season in autumn, the pier was built at the end of the 19th century, when Kinsale catches were exported as far as America. Now, the few commercial boats to be seen here, and at the two smaller slips we will pass on our route, bear sorry testament to the neglect and decline of fishing as an element of our local or national economy.

At the Trident Hotel, we reach World's End, as it is called locally, said to have been thus named by Viking longshipmen wintering there, far from home. The older people in the small, picturesque cottages on the hillside behind are held to have a different accent to other locals; it was, in fact a distinct community, very much linked to the sea. In the 17th century, naval dockyards were sited where the hotel now stands, with supplies of timber from the slopes above, Dromderrig, or The Hill of Oak Trees. Only in the 1960's were the basins filled in, making a car park for the Trident. The deepest water in the harbour is just offshore.

As we follow the pavement west along the water, the right side of the road is a deep cutting, made to accommodate the 'new' Bandon road, constructed in the mid-19th century. High above is Compass Hill, overlooking the harbour, and James Fort is on the spur of land known as Castle Park, opposite. Shots fired into James Fort from Compass Hill by a Cromwellian battery in 1649 forced the garrison to surrender.

Passing Ferryslip Quay, whence ferries once plied to Castle Park, and the Lobster Quay, a small pier, we may see the Rock of Oisín, mythologically connected with a hero of the ancient Fianna. However, it is covered at high tide. There are local otters, one of which frequents the moored fishing boats. In spring and summer, terns can been seen plummeting into the water after sprats. Their migrations may take them on a round trip from the Arctic to the Antarctic each year. The summer passage comprises tern families; the young birds may be heard calling to the parents, who feed them on the wing.

(2) We reach the 'new' bridge, Duggan Bridge, built in the 1970's to replace the Western Bridge, upstream. We do not cross it but continue along the water, past the car park and the quarry on the right where there are fine stands of gorse and ramparts as 'ivied' as any in a Tennyson poem. Across the estuary, the single gable of Ringrone Castle, once marking the boundaries of de Courcy territory, stands gaunt against the skyline.

The pavement conveniently skirts the water. Patently, it is a tidal estuary; bladderwrack weed grows on the mud beaches exposed at low tide, and oystercatchers and turnstones forage amongst it. The Bandon here is a fine, broad river, once a thoroughfare for boats delivering goods to the small quays along its banks. Until the 1960s, drift netting the river for salmon supported half a dozen local families but off-shore boats so decimated the fish that a total ban on river netting was imposed. Older folk at Ballinadee and Kilmacsimon Quay can point out the famous fishing holes and marks, each with its local name. Now, the Bandon is a river for sport anglers, one of the most important in Munster.

We shortly come to Commoge Marsh on the right. Soon, large painted plaques will illustrate the bird species, as identified and described by this author. Many of the migrant birds fly phenomenal distances to reach here, including godwits from Iceland and knot, from the Canadian High Arctic. The best time to watch is when the tide is low and the birds are roosting on

Commoge Marsh, with godwits

the mud. The alder and willow around the edges provide cover for nesting birds. The predators are our native hooded crow, raven, and magpie.

The marsh is a relatively recent phenomenon, created by the new road from Bandon to Kinsale, spanning, and partially damming, the mouth of Commoge Creek. It was constructed as a means of giving paid employment to the starving local population during the Great Famine of 1844/5/6. Previously, the entrance to the town from this side followed Cappagh Lane, two hundred yards beyond the creek, the route we will now take.

Cappagh Lane is almost hidden. On the sharp bend after the marsh, it, and a laneway to a house right on the corner, leave the road as one. It is a narrow, high-ditched lane, bounded by stone walls made in the Irish style of standing flat stones upon one another vertically rather than laying them horizontally, as elsewhere. These are now overgrown with a wonderful fecundity of moss, ivy, grasses and flowering plants. Navelworth is, of course, common, the round fleshy leaves dimpled at the centre; the tall flower, like a miniature foxglove but with small white 'bells', may shoot to a height of three feet. Foxgloves are in glorious purple flower in summer. Also, depending on the month, one will find primroses, Herb Robert, forget-me-not, dog violets and dog roses blooming along this lane. Such robust life is at odds with the tale that the lane is haunted. This story may have been initiated by smugglers who, using the lane to gain surreptitious access from the creek to the town, wished to discourage prying eyes and night walkers. Kinsale was notorious as a smugglers' haven, with wine from France and brandy from Spain.

As we ascend the lane - it is a moderate slope for all of a quarter of a mile - views over the marsh, river and harbour are available but it is worth waiting for the view from the top. Here, just past a line of new guest houses, there are turnings down to the right - Abbeycourt and, then, Harbour Heights - cul-de-sacs with broad lawns and 'terraces' from which one can look out over a panoramic view. Having contemplated it, we can retrace our steps to the road, and continue, past bungalows with African grasses and Cordylline palms - evidencing, as the estate agent might say, the "sub-tropical ambience" - until we turn right at the T-junction and descend towards the lovely town of Kinsale.

(3) We soon come upon a sign reminding us that Kinsale is twinned with those gems of the French Riviera, San Juan-les-Pins/Antibes. High quality, certainly, and perhaps the inspiration for the gourmet venue Kinsale has become today. The award for Best Kept Town is also noted, as is its sister-hood with Mumbles, the Gower Peninsula town of Dylan Thomas's child-hood. Other triumphs and distinctions of Kinsale are too many and too glorious to here mention.

Downhill, downhill, the town's roofscapes and steeples appearing below us, and when we see a line of toy town cottages on our right - "Mandeville Terrace, 1899" - we turn sharp left, uphill, and take the first right into Lower Catholic Walk, a fine promenade overlooking the town. This leads us to the Carmelite Friary church, an impressive building. The Carmelite Order has been associated with Kinsale, almost continuously, since 1334, ministering to the nearby leper hospital in the early years. In 1601, during the English attack on the Spanish occupied town, the earlier friary was blown asunder by guns on the hill above.

The tree-lined avenue that leads downhill from the front door of the present church is somewhat reminiscent of a small 'ramblas' in a Spanish town.

At the end, we turn right, into Cork Street, and immediately notice Desmond Castle. This was a

The remains of Ringrone Castle, with terns

Custom House built in the 16th century by the Earls of Desmond when offered the Custom dues of the port by the De Cogans, the local lords, who were somewhat nervous of their neighbours, the De Courcys, and hoped the Desmond's presence would protect them. In the event, the power of the

St. Multose Church

Desmonds ended with the last years of the century. Their vast Munster lands were confiscated by the English crown and allotted to such worthies as the 'gentle' poet, Edmund Spenser, and the courtier-adventurer, Sir Walter Raleigh.

In the 18th century, the Desmond Castle was a prison for French sailors taken on the high seas when England was at war with Napoleon. Here, a hapless 54 imprisoned men were burnt to death during a fire in 1747. Opposite the prison is the narrow Chairmans Lane, where sedan chair carriers queued for fares like a modern taxi rank and, apparently, quarrelled over clients. In this lane is also the cottage of the Kinsale Giant; it cannot have been easy for him to get through the door.

Past Desmond Castle, in the same street - which now becomes Friar Street - the imposing church of St. John the Baptist was erected in the new spirit of Catholic confidence after the Emancipation Act of 1829. It is an elegant building, in the classical style. The left turning almost opposite takes us to Church Street, where we turn left again, passing in front of Kinsale's most famous building, St. Multose Church.

(4) St Multose is immediately arresting in its appearance. Straight out of medieval Normandy, it is quite unlike the ancient churches we are familiar with in Ireland. It reminds us, more than other Norman ruins - there are

14

keeps, castles and pieces of castles in the countryside all around - of the 'Frenchness' of these invaders when they first came. It was built circa 1195, by Milo de Cogan, and designed like the stolid country churches of northern France. It has a second unique distinction; it has been a place of worship for an unbroken eight hundred years. The scale and openness of the interior, the ancient arches and the ironwork of the gates are all notable features. Many great events were celebrated here, including the 'crowning' or proclamation of King Charles II of England by Prince Rupert, who was blockaded in Kinsale when news of the execution of Charles I reached the town. In the event, the new king was not to be proclaimed in his English dominion until eleven years later.

We continue left along Church Street, and cross the junction into Market Place and Market Square. In 1600, the market house was built, a blockish house with arches in front to allow the easy access of goods and customers to the stalls and vendors within. In 1706, the hand-some loggia frontage was added, and a sec-ond floor which housed municipal offices. Here, the Sovereign of Kinsale - that is, the mayor - hosted corporation meetings and wel-

The Market House, with loggia

comed visitors. The medieval charters of the town are now held in the muse-um which has replaced these upstairs offices, while the toll boards displaying the tariffs charged to medieval traders may still be seen in the entrance log-gia.

A stroll down Market Quay returns us to our starting point in front of the Tourist Office. For post-walk relaxation, Kinsale, famous for its hostelries, offers many venues where a charming cup of tea or a pleasant 'warming drop' may be enjoyed.

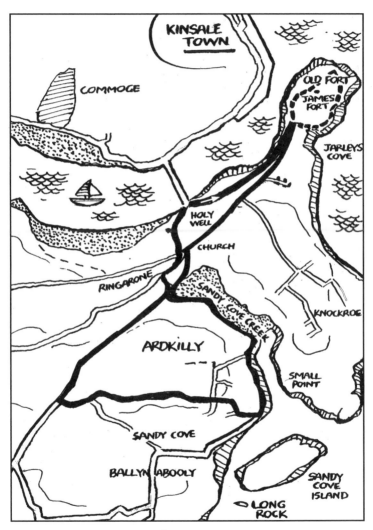

Walk No.2: James Fort. 1$\frac{1}{2}$ hrs or 3 hrs – 2 or 5 miles.

James Fort Walk

Duggan Bridge – Castle Park – James Fort – Ringarone – Sandy Cove – Ballymacaw Cross

Locality: OS Map Sheet 87 Squares 6347, 6348, 6448, 6449, about 1.5 miles south west of Kinsale.

Description and Distance: A loop walk with 2 options (A) 2 miles (B) 5 miles

Walking Time: including viewing the fort (A) 1 hr 30 mins (B) 3 hours

Walking conditions: Field paths, bohreens and back roads. One steep path (optional). 300 yards of the R600 – care should be taken at busy times.

Features: Postcard views of the inner harbour and town, their geographical features and ancient defences. A sense of wildness and antiquity at James Fort, the ruined castle and church. A bathing beach, sheltered 'fjord' side roads and an inshore island. A pretty sea side hamlet.

Flora and fauna: Kestrels, ravens, grey crows, stonechats, waders. Raucous bands of glossy-black choughs with red legs and beaks may be seen feeding in the cliff fields. Boxing hares are sometimes seen in early spring. Grey seals swim close in to the south shore of Castle Park. Kingfishers frequent the head of Sandy Cove Creek.

Equipment: In dry weather, everyday shoes but, after rain, the grassy paths around James Fort can be very wet.

Itinerary
Our starting point for this walk is the lay-by-cum-car-park at the opposite side of the Duggan Bridge from Kinsale town, about a mile west of the town centre.   One may reach this by taxi, car, bicycle or Shank's mare. Dedicated walkers may well chose the mare.

(1) A draught of bracing air, imbibed on the bridge span, is an excellent stimulant before setting out. In summer, anglers will be leaning over the parapet, fishing for mackerel when the shoals arrive on the tide. We cross the road

17

diagonally from the lay-by and set off down the water side, that is, the south side of the harbour. A pleasant walk of about a kilometre brings us to the small settlement of Castle Park. The name refers to an ancient structure on the site, across the harbour from Kinsale town.

As we walk, there are good views of the escarpment opposite, and the fine houses on its slopes. Small local fishing boats are often moored at the two piers. Kinsale is not the fishing port it once was; in the 15th century, it exported fish to Britain and France (see Town and Country Walk). Nowadays, trade-offs against agricultural subsides mean EU boats harvest Ireland's rich offshore waters while niggardly quotas and lack of investment mean Irish boats cannot compete.

We pass the Dock Pub, with tables outside in fine weather, and the small hamlet known as The Dock, the landing place for a cross-harbour ferry before the bridge was built. At the time of the Battle of Kinsale, 1601, there was a boat yard here. Great beams of iroko - ironwood - probably used to support boats during repairs, were recovered in recent times.

With the marina on our left, we pass a hostel and turn right past the gable of the last house. After climbing a few stone steps, we reach a pathway and turn left. The pathway climbs a little at first and crosses a stile where there is a finger-post indicating James Fort. The path is easy and well laid out, with excellent views over the mouth of the Bandon River where it meets the sea. The country is wild, with gorse, bracken and heather. Across the water is Kinsale, two small piers with fishing boats immediately opposite and a line of tiny 'toy town' cottages above, once no doubt cheap housing but now probably worth a fortune. Higher still are some fine Georgian houses in stately gardens. Further along, is the main Kinsale marina, with the town rising behind, a very beautiful town with tall, slim buildings climbing the hill and, off to the right, before Scilly woods, a line of apartment blocks, known locally as the Cash Registers for their resemblance to same and the profits they have engendered. All efforts by paint and plantation to camouflage or ameliorate their presence have so far proved unsuccessful.

Along the pathway, the stone wall is grown over with navelwort. The cushiony leaves - as big as a present day pound coin or an old penny, for which it was sometimes called "pennywort"- are fleshy discs of dark green with a depression at the centre, the 'navel'. The flowers, in July and August, are like miniature white foxgloves, a rising stalk of tiny thimbles, hanging like bells. Herb Robert, with bright red stalks and dark green leaves, is also abundant, called for Robert, an ancient Duke of Normandy who wrote a medical treatise, or, alternatively, for the fact that, being red, it was called "ruber" and was used to staunch the blood from wounds in medieval battles. Also, there

James Fort, built a year after the Battle of Kinsale

is hart's-tongue fern, shiny green and like the long, pointed tongue of a hart, or deer, and hard fern, and spleenwort and wall rue. With yellow and grey lichens, primroses, violets, foxgloves, monbretia and garlic-smelling ransoms, the walls along this walk are a potpourri of smells and colours in spring and summer time.

(2) To our right, now, are the ramparts of James Fort. One may climb these now - they are more like earth mounds than walls - or enter, later, by a gate known as The Drawbridge, which we will pass on the south side. A platform, along which sentries might patrol, runs all around the top of the ramparts and so makes a tour a relatively easy matter. The views are wonderful, with nearby Kinsale town to the north, the pretty village of Summer Cove and monolithic Charles Fort due east across the harbour, the opening to the sea southwards, and the broad meanders of the River Bandon to the west.

James Fort was begun in 1602, a year after the Battle of Kinsale, at the expense of the townspeople in return for the restoration of the town's charter. The cost was not only a 'fine' imposed on them for their collusion with the Spaniards, but also ensured that protection against any future Catholic 'invasion' was paid for by the Irish themselves. Strategically, the site was perfect, overlooking the harbour mouth and on high ground almost surrounded by water but for the narrow isthmus at the Dock bar. Built on the site of the earlier "Chastell Parke" - which had been occupied by the Spaniards in 1601 - the construction was 'state-of-the-art' for the times with, probably, the first use of bastions in Irish fortification.

Mr John Thullier, in his excellent "History of Kinsale", describes the five bastions as being joined by earthworks, with a dry moat outside. Where there was stone facing, much of it was later purloined for use by local builders. Inside the bastions and ramparts was another fort, with walls five metres high and, within this, two square towers, with battlements and bastions, the last line of defence.

Passing the fort on one's right, one enters a large, green field with a ruin at the end. It is worth pausing at this ruin to enjoy the magnificent view. Below, the land falls sharply away to a stone fort, The Blockhouse,' on the edge of the water. The path that leads down to it - around the ruin's gable - can be slippery in wet weather, like a muddy Cresta Run. Reasonable caution is required to avoid tobogganing into the building below.

(3) The Blockhouse, built long before the fort, in 1549, allowed emplaced cannon to rake the channel at point-blank range. From here, a defensive iron chain was sometimes floated to the other shore, barring entry to the harbour at night or in times of danger. The floor is of bedrock, and the stone struc-

Kestrels at Castle Park

ture is roughly semicircular. The arched windows, latticed with iron bars, look across at colourful Summer Cove and the massive grey bulk of Charles Fort, rising out of the sea.

Emerging, and before retracing one's steps, with some effort, up the 'Cresta Run', it is worth climbing the scalp of bare rock immediately to the left and enjoying the fine view down the coastline between the headlands of the bay. On a hot day, it might be tempting to scramble down a rough path through the furze to the sea but we are shortly to come to a small sand beach where a pause for a quick dip might be more comfortable, and safer. Having trudged up the path which we slithered down, we pass the ruin again on our right and continue towards some other ruins straight ahead; these are the remains of the inner fort of James Fort. In springtime, we can look out to sea over acres of flowering gorse and blackthorn. As mentioned elsewhere, blackthorn flowers

The Blockhouse

turn into leaves, and the fruit is sloes, excellent for making sloe gin or sloe 'poteen'. In the case of whitethorn, or may blossom, the flowers, often pink, appear later and turn into haws, the red meaty berries beloved of birds and Irish country children walking to school. However, I must warn my readers not to try them at my behest, for fear they might eat the wrong berries, and expire.

Stonechats, neat little birds, the males with black heads, white collars and chestnut breasts, the females similar but less showy, are common here, standing prominently on briars or fence wires to sing. The call is said to resemble two pebbles struck together, hence the name. Yellowhammers may also be seen, the cocks as bright as canaries, singing their song, "A little bit of bread and no cheese". It is tragic that this attractive bird is disappearing everywhere, hedgerow loss being, in large part, the cause. With luck, one may spot a merlin - which eats yellowhammers - scudding low over the heath land, fast as a fleeting shadow, glimpsed and then gone. The wall beside the pathway is rich in mosses and wayside plants, especially foxgloves, tall stalks of purple flowers, many fingers and no thumbs.

(4) Now reaching, again, the ramparts of James Fort, the path divides into three, to right and left following the dry moat outside the ramparts and, in the

Salmon, once an industry on the Bandon River

centre, climbing the ramparts. The centre path takes us to the ruins, with stone buildings, as mentioned in (2), above. We enter and explore the ruins and, then, with the ruins on our right, pass via the Drawbridge, a stone-faced cutting through the ramparts, to the moat outside. To the left, a bastion, riddled with rabbit burrows and splashed with primroses, blocks our way: we go right, following the moat and climb via a gap in the wall to a path outside the structure. This leads back to The Dock and Castle Park, following a well-worn path that diverges from the ramparts and descends diagonally across the field towards a line of evergreen "palms", so-called locally because the leaves are blessed in the church on Palm Sundays. Just before the sea, the path turns right through a stile and leads onto a small beach. We cross the top of this pleasant beach - the lawn that abuts it is marked "Private Garden" - and exit on the other side, where we follow a path between hedges returning us in front of the Dock bar.

(5) We turn left; the road forks; we go left, climbing the hill. This road ascends gradually, but steadily, to high ground with extensive views over the mouth of the Bandon River and the "new" Duggan Bridge. Ignoring a road to the left, we continue to the top, where a path through a graveyard on the right of the road leads to the ruined church of Courtmaher, the 'mother

church'. While closely connected with the Norman family, De Courcy - Myles De Courcy was first Baron of Kinsale in 1223 - a tradition holds that St Patrick departed from here to visit Rome and, indeed, a local church is held to pre-date St Patrick. Little remains now but the ruins, with the De Courcy castle of Ringrone reduced to a single stalwart gable standing in the nearby field.

Returning to the road, we descend steeply to a signpost indicating "Sandy Cove 1 mile" . Here, we have two options: (A) We may take a short route back to our starting point at Duggan Bridge. If we chose this 'short option', we turn right, uphill, and twenty yards along, at the T-junction, turn right again. After five hundred yards, we are back at the bridge. This route is described in the last paragraph of this piece. (B) We may continue the walk to Sandy Cove village and island.

(6) To reach Sandy Cove village, we do not turn right uphill, but go straight ahead, down to the shores of a small inlet, Sandy Cove Creek. Here, a stone bridge crosses the creek at a hairpin bend. In winter, we are likely to see redshank - with red legs - and greenshank - with green legs - probing the shallows, a grey heron or two fishing along the shore and a few black-and-white oystercatchers with orange beaks stepping about the shingle. This creek is seasonally full of sand gobies, small plaice and small eels. Kingfishers are resident here and, with luck, one may see one fishing from a perch protruding above the water.

The road now follows the southern shore of the inlet, with the water on the left, to the small hamlet of Sandy Cove. This, with flowering blackthorn in spring or orange montbretia and sweet smelling honeysuckle in summer, is a pleasant rural walk, with a tang of the sea. Soon

Foxgloves, in July

Ringrone Castle

after "The Pill", a small island across the channel from the village, comes into view, a road climbs steeply to the right. We will be taking this road, but might first like to explore the pleasant little settlement just a few hundred yards along. Swimming to the island is popular with local youth - it is almost possible to walk across at low tide. The island is the home of a herd of wild goats, beloved of Sandy Cove residents. A cliff side walk extends to an old chapel beyond the village but, unfortunately, does not make a 'round'.

(7) The road we take is, as aforementioned, to the right just before the hamlet. It is usually signposted "Kinsale Language Centre" but, in Ireland, signposts sometimes change. It doubles back on the coast road and rises steeply. We climb for the first ten minutes, with magnificent views down the coast, past Hake Head to the Old Head of Kinsale. From here, it seems there are two hazy headlands in the distance, each with a 'tower'. In fact, both promontories are part of The Old Head, the nearer building being one of the line of coastal signal towers built to guard against a French invasion, circa 1796, and the further, five miles away from us, the lighthouse at the tip. The Old Head is steeped in history, pre-history and legend, and was a naturalist's paradise until it was extensively developed as a private golf course in the mid-1990's, and the old vegetation of the cap was replaced by, largely, non-native species. Previously, it had provided walkers, fishermen, geologists and Sunday strollers access to a dramatic and unspoiled wilderness only 20 miles from Cork city. The Old Head may still be walked but now only upon payment of

an admission fee, and walkers must stay on the marked paths. Those interested in golf landscaping will admire the transformation of rude wilderness into manicured fairways; it is, now, a very fine golf course. The headland reaches out into the sea and is often the first landfall for migrant birds crossing the Bay of Biscay; at night the light is a further guide. Tired arrivals from Spain and Africa rest there before following the course of the Bandon River into the hinterland.

Reaching a T-junction at Ballymacaw Cross Roads, we turn right. The road soon begins to descend steeply, with the land falling away to the left and the R600 road on the opposite side of the valley. Stands of purple loosestrife edge the verge in summer, along with many ferns and fuschia bushes, while honeysuckle drapes the trees which form a tunnel around us as we go steeply down towards the creek, below.

Arriving at the headwaters of the creek, we go straight ahead and now must retrace our earlier route for a few hundred yards. At the Sandy Cove signpost which we passed earlier, we go left uphill - as described in the 'short option' (A) above - and immediately meet the main road, the R600, where we turn right towards Kinsale. This is an awkward stretch of road when there is heavy traffic - however, we soon leave it. The stump of Ringarone stands high above the slope overgrown with gorse, brambles and the white, trumpet-like flowers of bindweed. Below us, on the left, is the Bandon River. We shortly arrive back at Duggan Bridge and our starting point.

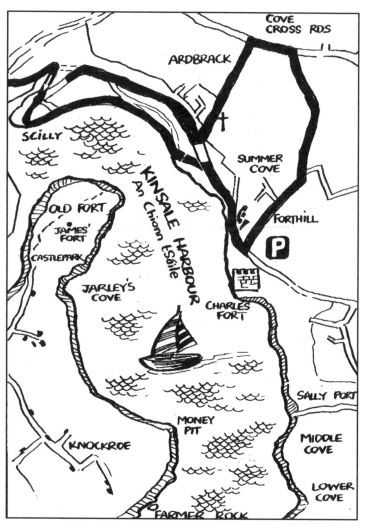

Walk No.3: Scilly and Charles Fort. 2 hours. About 4 miles.

Scilly and Charles Fort Walk

The east shore of Kinsale Harbour - Lower Road and Scilly Walk - Summer Cove - Charles Fort - Ringacurra - High Road - Breakheart Hill

Locality: OS Map Sheet 87 Squares 6450, 6550 and 6549, beginning and ending at Kinsale Post Office.

Description and Distance: A loop walk, about 4 miles

Walking Time: 2 hours, plus an hour at Charles Fort.

Walking conditions: Tarred paths and roads. One short, steep climb.

Features: The harbour and town viewed from water level and from high above. Panoramic vistas over the inner harbour, and Castle Park 'island' and James Fort. The whole of the Bandon estuary and harbour system may be seen, from the Bandon mouth, at Duggan Bridge, to the harbour mouth at Money Point, then over the sea to the lighthouse on the Old Head of Kinsale.

Flora and fauna: The focus of this walk is scenery and history. Cormorants and mute swans will be seen in the harbour, along with common and herring gulls, black-headed, great black-back and lesser black-back gulls. Herons, oystercatchers and redshanks may be present at low tide. The old woods along the Scilly Walk will be of interest to tree watchers, and to bird watchers in search of warblers in summer.

Equipment: Everyday shoes.

Itinerary
Leaving the Post Office in the centre of town, we follow the pavement to the left, past the supermarket and under the decorative iron balconies of the Perryville House Hotel. The road divides at a Y junction. We take the lower road, following the water. There is excellent car parking just before the hairpin bend where the road turns right and climbs. On the corner, there is a green space, and a spring known as Scilly Well. Here, we begin the walk.

(1) Behind Scilly Well, a path leads into Deasy's Bog, wet ground earmarked

27

as a wildlife park, another attraction soon to be added to the attractive town. A sign post announces "Featherbed Lane" and "Breakheart Hill"; we will be returning via the latter and the story behind these names can then be told. Meanwhile, we round the hairpin and begin the gentle climb up the pavement on the left side of the road. We pass a small garden, with seats and a limestone block carved with the word "Scilly". This, the name of the area, may come from the Irish word for the flexible sally branches used in the construction of lobster pots. A more imaginative, or silly, proposition is that it was the home of a colony of refugee smugglers from the Scilly Isles.

We continue along the gable of The Spaniards Inn. Kinsale quite legitimately makes much of its connection with Spain. On October 2nd 1601, an army of 4,000 Spaniards landed and took control of Kinsale, Castle Park and Ringrone (see Brown's Mills Walk). In November, an English force of 7,500 besieged the town. In December, a large Irish force under O'Neill and O'Donnell of Ulster marched the length of Ireland in atrocious weather and deployed behind the English lines. Despite the advantage of greater numbers, because of impetuosity the Irish and Spanish were defeated. In the Battle of Kinsale, the last hopes for Ireland were lost. It signalled the end of the old Irish world, of the Gaelic lordships, and a distinctive way of life.

As we come to The Spaniards corner, we do not round it but continue straight across, down a road descending to the water, affording views of the terraced town, the grey bulk of the Mercy Convent pre-eminent. At the water, there is a boat slip, piled with lobster pots and ropes; in the past, Scilly was a fishing community, and small boat fishermen still moor here. The attractively extended houses once knew more humble occupants. Now, the Scilly waterfront is a prime location in the town. Many yachts are moored at the marina opposite. Once, commercial fishing in Kinsale was so bustling that one could cross the harbour walking on berthed boats from Scilly to Pier Head.

(2) The narrow street turns left and we pass The Spinnaker public house. The balconies and picture windows of the houses on both sides vie for harbour views, and we can see why Kinsale is compared with Cornish villages. Across the water, Castle Park 'island' is in clear view, with James Fort, the ruined church and the Blockhouse - but these ruins will be a constant presence on this Lower Road walk and we will enjoy spectacular prospects at a later stage. Meanwhile, the terrestrial view ahead is the shocking pinks, pastel greens and powder blues of the Ardbrack Heights apartment blocks, otherwise known as 'The Cash Registers' (see James Fort walk). In contrast, we may wish to rest our eyes on the lovely yellow house deep in the woods ahead, or the pier and stately frontages of Summer Cove, or the great grey ramparts of Charles Fort, rising above the sea.

Oystercatchers, at low tide

On fine days, yachts in full sail cruise the calm waters beside us, and flotillas of swans paddle in the shallows. A road arrives from the left and, now, a terrace of small houses face one another on either side of our route. We pass a sign saying "Cul de sac". Steps lead down to the weedy shore.

The narrow roadway runs alongside, and twenty feet above, the water. After 150 yards, a wicket, on the left, accesses a leafy pathway to the road above. We continue along the water, passing seats where old gentlemen

Entrance to Charles Fort, with harbour mouth

sometimes sit and contemplate the town, and a colourful ancient pump on our right. The mouth of the harbour comes into view, then the open sea and, in the opposite direction, Duggan Bridge and the Bandon River.

This is a lovely, leafy walk, with a substantial grove on the slopes to the left and the yellow house in the woods ahead, with the path passing in front of and below it. I once saw a juvenile long eared owl staring at me from the shadows of the high canopy. When I pointed it out to friends, they thought I was truly a champion bird watcher. In fact, it happened completely by chance. Raising my binoculars to look for chiffchaffs, I found the owl in the lens. The path shortly veers slightly left and climbs to the tarred road just above the village of Summer Cove.

(3) The walk downhill to Summer Cove is truly enchanting. The roadway is narrow with small, pretty houses, gaily painted, on either side. While the comparison with Cornish villages or sea front hamlets like Dylan Thomas's village in "Under Milk Wood" may be made, this street has a Gallician flavour - perhaps it is the balconies, the shuttered windows and the paint.

At sea level, we have a boat slip and the Bulman pub, called for a rock off the east shore and a buoy hung with bells that tolled a warning when the sea got rough. A car park now occupies what was once a quay. This is a very pleasant place to pause and survey the town to the right, James Fort and the Blockhouse, opposite, and the bulk of Charles Fort just down the shore to the left. We face a steep, but very short, climb out of the village and up the hill ahead.

(4) Fort Hill is steep, but well worth it. Reaching the flat summit, we have top-of-the-world views over the harbour mouth, the Atlantic, the Old Head of Kinsale and Bream Rock. Charles Fort is open to the public from mid-April to October, with an exhibition and guided tours. The admission fee is modest, and worthwhile.

The fort is like a huge block of sharp-cornered stone, stolid, squat, apparently impregnable, at least from the sea where it rises from the shoreline rocks in massive bulwarks and bastions. A 'five pointed bastion fort', so categorised, it was built in 1680 as part of the elaborate defences of the town, nervous of a sea attack by Louis XIV of France. It is considered one of the finest examples surviving. The name was changed from Ringcurran to Charles Fort by the British, in honour of King Charles II of England, first proclaimed at St Multose Church, Kinsale in 1649 (see Town and Country Walk). It was attacked from land by William of Orange's generals in 1690, the moat on the landward side providing no defence from guns on the higher ground above. Over the centuries, Kinsale was an important Royal Navy base and the fortress continued in use by British forces until 1921.

(5) Opposite Charles Fort, and signposted "Cork", is a road worth taking, a quiet country road affording yet higher views over the sea. Now, not only the lighthouse on the Old Head is visible, but the ruined Signal Tower at the landward end. Also, James Fort, with Duggan Bridge and the Bandon mouth behind it, and the sloping fields in forty shades of green. This road has an inland peace about it. I have seen yellowhammers here, an increasing rare bird, a merlin, once, and small charms of goldfinches.

At the T-junction, we go left, and take the next left about 200m along. There is a brown finger post, indicating a church and a pine tree. Indeed, it's surprising accurate, for this is what we will come upon just down the road.

We pass a sign, "Drive slowly through the village", although we encounter no village but, rather, walk down a tree lined road, noticing a remarkable carved capstone on a plain gate pier on the left. Next, on the right, a fine weather slated Georgian house, with a graceful, shallow fanlight and beautifully proportioned windows on each of the two floors. After that, it is Irish

St Catherine's Church, Ringacurra

bungalows, some pretty, some plain, then a terrace of new houses and, just below it, St. Catherine's Church of Ireland church, a quaint little edifice almost 200 years old, set amongst trees.

(6) At the T-junction, we turn right. On the outward leg, we used the Lower Road by the water; we are taking the High Road home. Now, ahead of us all the way, we have magnificent views over harbour and town. Few sites in Kinsale afford better.

The views need little commentary; we have mentioned the features all before. But, now, there is the pleasure of recognition, and overview. We see how the town fits together, terracing down from the hills to the sheltered harbour, how the great Bandon River carved its path between the rounded bulk of Castle Park and the steep escarpments on the north side above Duggan Bridge. It is a fine view, especially fine as the western sun falls on the port in the evening, and we walk west towards the sun. The moored boats, the fishing boats and sail boats coming and going, the town rising behind combine in a classical, almost chocolate box, picture. The elevation adds a very pleasant effect indeed.

We now have only one last landmark to watch for to make this walk a loop. On the right side, 300m before the Spaniards corner, there are fat black and yellow bollards and a tarred path descending steeply and providing a short route down to Scilly Well, our starting point. If one passes a sign on the left indicating "Scilly Walking Tour", one has gone 200m too far.

This steep path is the aforementioned Breakheart Hill. At Scilly Well, a path climbs up the opposite slope and reaches the R600 road to Cork, which it crosses. This is known as Featherbed Lane because Kinsale girls, wooed by British soldiers serving at Charles Fort and living in the military housing just off the lane, were seduced there. Later, finding them pregnant, their feckless lovers would bid them good-bye on Breakheart Hill.

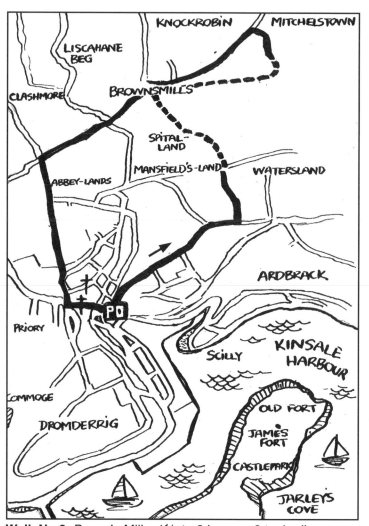

Walk No.3: Brown's Mills. 1½ to 2 hours – 3 to 4 miles.

Brown's Mills Walk

Out of town via The Glen - Watersland - Oysterhaven Creek - Brown's Mills - Clasheen Cross - return to town via Friar's Gate

Locality: OS Map Sheet 87 Squares 6350, 6450, 6451, 6351, etc. , beginning and ending at Kinsale Post Office.

Description and Distance: A loop walk, 3 to 4 miles.

Walking time: 1 hr 30 mins but, at leisure, 2 hrs.

Walking conditions: After heavy or prolonged rain, provision should be made for muddy conditions on the green lanes, and long wet grass.

Features: Green lanes and quite country roads. The headwaters of Oysterhaven Creek, the quiet historic hamlet of Brown's Mills. Places associated with the Battle of Kinsale, 1601, the English Camp, etc. A Famine graveyard.

Flora and fauna: The flora is copious, with the roadside hedges and ditches a botanist's delight. It is well worth carrying a wildflower field guide in spring or summer.   The sheltered green lanes are host to many butterflies. Rabbits may well be seen, or hares in the creek side fields in March and April. Rarer hedgerow birds include stonechats and yellowhammers, with flocks of redwing and fieldfares in winter.

Equipment: Waterproof shoes may be necessary in wet weather.

Itinerary
(1) Exit the Post Office, turning right. We turn right again at the Blue Haven, at the top of the street. This takes us up The Glen for a hundred yards. Before the land between it and the sea was reclaimed, The Glen was a dock serving the inner harbour, with warehouses and bondhouses on the water.   Sedan chairmen were available for hire at nearby Chairman's Lane, perhaps to carry portly or drunken captains to lodgings in the steep streets above.   At the end of The Glen, we reach Brewery Corner, once the site of Cuckoo Mill where corn was ground and rape seed pressed for oil to keep the light of the Old

Old farm shed, Mitchelstown, Kinsale

Head beacon burning. Passing the Fire Station, we ascend the steep hill to the right. Although only minutes from town, this road has a country feel to it. We pass a "Yield" sign, where a road enters from the right, and continue, passing St Multouse School. We reach Henry Good's Mill, on our left. Here, we may pause to look back at fine views of the inside harbour.

(2) The road is now wide. Passing the mill on our left, we are now, definitely, 'in the country'. Just before a large guest house, "Waterlands", a narrow lane turns down to the left. Tar macadam persists for a few hundred yards, with a house or two; then the way is gravelled; then it becomes a grassy track.

(3) The track descends steeply between bushes of flowering blackthorn and may-blossom in spring, with primroses and violets in profusion along the banks. Later, these are replaced by tall foxgloves and the bushes, then green, are bedecked in honeysuckle. There is a stand of tall, golden Evening Primrose half way down, and a watercourse which may make the going soggy. In winter, the bushes bear haws and sloes, and redwings and field-fares, thrushes arriving ravenous from the Scandinavian winter, descend upon them to gorge their fill. They are nervous birds, and fly ahead of us from tree to tree. Bullfinches are also a feature of this green road, flitting from bush to bush, easily spotted by their brilliant white rump. The male, with black cap over a swollen scarlet chest, and the female, with black cap and chocolate brown breast, make one of the handsomest pairs in the king-dom of hedgerow birds.

There will be glimpses of the head-waters of Oysterhaven Creek below us to the right; when the trees are bare, there will be views. In winter, this path may be wet in places, and one should be careful not to slip on the wet grass. Where the way is rough or slippery, wise walkers do not proceed with hands in pockets. It is better to break one's fall with one's palms than with one's nose.

At the bottom of the track, we pass Creek Guest House, positioned prettily amongst trees, and reach the small, tarred road at Brown's Mills. Here, grouped around the creek head, is an attractive hamlet of old stone houses, a country pub - Katie's Lounge Bar - and a large stone building, the eponymous mill. This, a 3-storey water mill built in 1700 and until recently in ruins, is now under sympathetic renovation. As we emerge onto the road a sign opposite informs us that in 1601, during the Battle of Kinsale, ships arrived here at the head of Oysterhaven Creek with supplies and reinforcements for the besieging English army. A sign outside the mill indicates that the English camp was only half a mile away.

(4) Beyond Katie's, is a brightly painted small cottage, with a footbridge in the front garden. There is a right turn alongside it. We take this and cross a small, stone bridge. A grassy path leads right, to the creek head. Follow this. A heap of fish nets and coloured fish boxes lie beside the hedge. When the tide is out, a small channel winds between the gravel and mud banks, with emerald green weed swirling in the slow current, like long tresses of hair. Herons fish in the shallows, and redshank and curlew stalk the mud. This stream holds the fry of flatfish, and small eels, in summer. Gently lift a stone,

and a fish will dart out in a flurry of sand. Glittering dragonflies and damselflies are attracted by the water. They spend their first two years of life as freshwater nymphs, preying upon insects, tadpoles and small fish. In adulthood, they lay their eggs in water, and hawk for insects over the surface.

Georgian house and treelined drive, Knockrobbin

In early summer, white lilac on the ditches greets the walker to this old roadway. It is now a quiet green lane, climbing gently, occasionally used by tractors and often muddy after wet weather. Up to about twenty years ago, it was a Council maintained road, and the owners of the first house along it, with the lovely gardens, recall its use for car rallies at that time.

Beyond the briary hedges, fulsome with fat blackberries in a good summer, fields slope down to the shores of the creek. The laneway, on a sunny day, is idyllic, reminiscent of childhood summers with butterflies everywhere -

speckled woods, red admirals, painted ladys - and the drone of carder, bumble and honey bees. Cow parsley and angelica grows along the ditches - also, some hogweed, which should be avoided because it raises painful weals on the skin.

At the top of the lane, there is a tin roofed shed and a gateway on the right affording a fine view of the new bridge on the R600 and a sweep of new blacktop highway below. Both Oysterhaven Creek and the Belgooly River are visible in the wide panorama from this high place.

The next twenty or more yards can be very difficult in wet weather, when the path is boggy or a large pool collects. Beyond it, the path climbs, and arrives at a gate, with an old whitewashed, slated shed on the right. The gate should be carefully closed after we pass through.

A large, detached 1950s or 1960s house stands in a raised garden on the left. On the right, we pass a classical Irish farmyard, low, whitewashed buildings on two-and-a-half sides. It is now in disuse. The gable of one thick walled white outhouse has ruptured down its length and the clay mortar of a bygone age clearly shows. So, also, does the old thatch under the tin roof, red with rust. But this lovely yard is private property, and should not be trespassed upon. The pathway continues, and passes another long, low house gable on the right before it reaches a T-junction at a narrow, tarred road.

(5) We are on top of a hill, between Knockrobin and Mitchelstown. There are modern bungalows on the road to our right. We turn left and pass the concrete enclosure of a wayside water pump, now gone, and set off downhill. This is a lovely road, narrow, with overgrown hedges and burgeoning fecundity, a botanist's feast. Glimpses are to be had of the creek below, and the gorse banks on the other side. Harts'-tongue ferns grow to prodigious lengths in the shelter of the high ditches. On the left, we have blackthorn, whitethorn and ash; on the right, big trees, ash, beech, sycamore and field maple shading the road. It is a sun-dappled, old fashioned road, reminiscent of a Constable painting. So quiet is the scene that we often see rabbits grazing in the roadside fields, or cock pheasants strutting about the winter plough land.

On the right, large gate piers and a sweeping entrance lead down a driveway to an elegant Georgian house with a fine fanlight and five windows on the first floor. In summer, cows, lying in the meadow in front, are almost hidden by the long grass. A view of Brown's Mill, in the valley, is to be had at the entrance. Just below, is a small lodge, with roses draping its impressive stone gateway. At the bottom of the slope, we pass the creek-side pathway we took earlier, and re-cross the bridge to come out again facing Brown's Mills.

(**6**) Now, turning left, we briefly retrace our steps past Katie's pub. An uphill road must now be climbed, steep but short. At the top, at Pike Cross, we come to a main road, the R607. Before crossing it, we may pause to read the plaque on the left which tells us that this high ground was the site of the English camp in 1601, with a force of 6,600 foot and 650 horse under Mountjoy besieging the Spanish force of 4,000 in Kinsale (see Scilly and Charles Fort Walk). The Irish army, under O'Neill, was encamped about three miles north. The English camp then straddled what was the old road to Cork. There was a turnpike, or toll gate here once, hence the name "Pike Cross".

We enter the small road almost opposite the plaque. This would have been the route taken by English forces to the battle site. It is a quiet country road, climbing slightly, with a few houses on the right. We cross the route of the old railway and, at the next cross, turn left onto the R605, going slightly downhill towards the town. At a left turning, signposted "Hospital", we go straight ahead, taking the sign for "Kinsale". We are now on a road called "The Rock". The hospital, to our left, was originally a Workhouse for the destitute. The road crosses the site of the old burial grounds. A limestone plaque commemorates the site as "An Poll Buí, The Great Famine 1845-1995". The date is, of course, confusing, but the name "An Poll Buí" means "The Yellow Hole", so called because so many starving and cholera-stricken bodies were interred there. A memorial cross stands in an area of mown grass, entered via a white gate and stile.

At the top of the hill, we have our first glimpses of Kinsale, below us. Now, as we descend, we may enjoy wide panoramas of the multicoloured houses, the fine harbour with yachts in sail, and the salient of Castle Park against the rising countryside beyond. We enter the town via The Friary Gate, an ancient town gate through which Carmelite friars walked from their abbey lands, close by. Father Matthew, the Apostle of Temperance, passed triumphantly through this gate, lead by bands and sober crowds, in 1844.

The descending road curves gently left towards the town centre with St Multose Church (see Town and Country Walk) straight ahead. In front of it, we go left, and this brings us into the Market Square. Rounding the Market House, with the ancient anchor against the wall, we emerge in Pearse Street, opposite the Blue Haven. Our starting point, the Post Office, is just down the street.

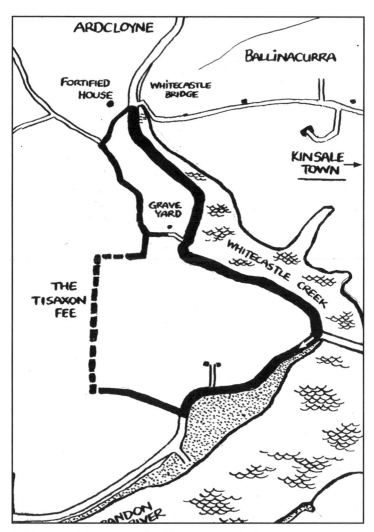

Walk No.5: Tisaxon and White Castle. Under 2 hours – 3 miles.

Tisaxon and White Castle Walk

The north bank of the Bandon above the new bridge - The Fee and Tisaxon – Whitecastle or Ballinacurra Creek

Locality: OS Map Sheet 87 Squares 6150, 6049, 6050, beginning a mile west of Kinsale town.

Description and Distance: A loop walk, 3 miles

Walking Time: under 2 hours

Walking conditions: Quiet tar macadam roads and green roads. No steep climbs.

Features: The broad estuary of the lovely Bandon River, with creeks and inlets. Remains of the old western bridge. Grassy lanes between fields. The site of two Neolithic Fulachta Fian. A ruined church and old graveyard. The ruin of a fortified house.

Flora and fauna: Along the verges, wild flowers thrive in profusion. Outstanding in early spring are the ramsons, then followed by the cycle of bluebells, buttercups, oxeye daisies and foxgloves, but many more flowers will be found, some rare or local. Mats of primroses, interspersed with dog violets, are common on the mossy banks of the green lanes. Water birds are the principal fauna on this river side walk. Of the ducks, mallard and shel-duck may be seen all year, with teal and widgeon in winter. Kingfishers are often seen on Ballinacurra Creek. Little egret, very rare until 1990, is increas-ingly common. The species established a   nesting colony on the Blackwater, in east Cork, in 1997 and raised 20 young.   Other waders include heron, black tailed godwit, redshank, greenshank, curlew and lapwing. Cormorants are regular. Migrants follow the Bandon River inland. Rabbits are common in the fields, with occasional hares and foxes seen early in the morning.

Equipment: Water resistant, rather than heavy-duty, shoes are advisable if walking this route after rain.

Itinerary

The starting point of this walk is west of Kinsale town. Enthusiastic trampers may choose to reach this point on foot from the town, via Cappagh Lane (Town and Country Walk) but will almost double the distance. Those motoring or cycling to the starting point should leave Kinsale on the R600, travelling west along the waterfront to Duggan Bridge, on the Bandon River. We do not cross the bridge, but continue upriver on the R606 - the river is on our left. We pass Commoge Marsh (Town and Country Walk) on the right, and reach a low stone bridge, more of a causeway. Immediately we cross it, there is a signpost indicating Clonakilty, Inishannon and Bandon. We take the left turning, marked Cul de Sac. There is a green Post Box on the corner. This is the starting point for the Tisaxon/White Castle walk.

(1) The roadside is resplendent with wildflowers; I have found relative rarities, such as Prostrate Toadflax, along it. In April, it is white with ramsons for a half mile on both sides. Ramsons are often called 'wild garlic', and they emanate a pungent, onion-like smell. The milk of cows that eat it is tainted. The flower heads are brilliant white and star-like, the leaves like those of lily-of-the-valley. 'Rams' may derive from an old word meaning rank; the

Shelduck over Bandon river

Linnean name means 'bear's garlic'. Richard Mabey, in his classic "Food For Free" , tells us that the leaves, when cooked, can be used for flavouring. He has - admirably - found ways of eating almost everything that grows wild, and still survives. There are good views across the Bandon, particularly attractive when the banks opposite are aflame with gorse. Up to the 1970s, the Bandon was drift-netted by local boats and the plentiful salmon that were taken provided a living for a dozen families. In the river's lore, every creek and rock was known and named, and famous fishing 'marks' were celebrated. However, as salmon stocks dwindled, netting was prohibited; it was reckoned £1,000 of tourist revenue accrued for every pound of salmon caught with rod and line. Thus, although it was not so much the traditional netters in the rivers as the new monofilament nets used at sea that threatened the salmon's survival, all river netting was stopped. Now, the increase in pig units and agricultural run-off threatens the rivers more than the netsmen ever did, and controls will have to urgently be applied.

Walking west in the afternoon, the light on the river is very beautiful. We see the stump of the old bridge, the Western Bridge, on the opposite side. Tisaxon House, up to our right, is weather slated, a somewhat unusual feature in the Irish countryside, but not uncommon in Kinsale town. The river bank is like a seashore, with bladderwrack seaweed, oystercatchers and gulls. A mixed flock of finches twitters from bush to bush along the lane ahead of us, goldfinches with yellow wing bars and red and white faces, blue-pink chaffinches and greenfinches in lime green.

We are to take the second turning right, just before a cottage on the roadside - but it is worth initially passing the entrance to this road and continuing for a hundred yards to see the stump of the old Western Bridge and the wreck of a boat, big-bellied and broad beamed, lying on its side in the mud. The bridge, replaced by Duggan Bridge, is of solid stone; we can see its companion stump on the other bank. Opposite, also, we can see Curahoo Creek, Curahoo House on high land above it.

On the road beyond this bridge, there are fine houses with secluded and exclusive views over the river. This is an affluent river-

Egret, new to Ireland

side enclave. The Kinsale which, in my childhood, was a dusty, dilapidated backwater has become one of the most favoured roosts in Ireland for the rich, especially Americans, who savour its quaintness and character. Ballymacwilliam House, happily not overly 'restored', lies beyond, up a private road. Once the manor house, it is now the home of a successful pop musician.

(2) Retracing our steps a hundred yards, we take the right turn mentioned earlier, now, of course, on our left. This is a private road upon which the owner - see "To the farmers and landowners" at the front of the book - kindly allows us passage. There is a modern bungalow on the right, after which the tar macadam gives way to a gravelled road. There is a fuschia hedge on the left and a field with a few old vehicles on our right. We arrive at an attractive farmhouse with dormer windows and a cement yard in front and, without disturbing the owners' privacy, skirt around it, to the right. Some care should

be taken to avoid a wet patch outside the gate of the farmyard behind the house.

Now greened over, the path of the old road is clear, running directly north, with the left hand ditch intact most of the way. We meet electric fences across the lane here and there, and get under or over them depending upon our size and agility. The ground may be churned up by cattle in winter, but we can seek the high sides of the path and avoid the mud. It would be interesting to 'age' the hedgerow - and thus, possibly, the road - by counting the number of shrub species it contains per thirty yards. According to Hooper's Hypothesis *(M D Hooper, British botanist, writing in 1974)* a hedge will have one shrub species for every one hundred years it has existed, averaged by sampling along 30 yard lengths.

Looking back, we can see the Bandon River behind us to the right, and to the left, wooded Whitecastle Creek.

(3) At the end of a field, we climb over an electric fence and a fallen gate and follow the path, right, down a narrow green lane, with the creek visible a few fields, below. Shortly, the path turns left and we are again going north. Now, the route is clearly an old roadway. On the walls at either side, quite large trees are established, sycamore and ash, forming a corridor of green shade. Here and there, bushes and briars - with delicious blackberries in late summer - have invaded the route but it is quite passable down the centre.

We shortly reach the wreck of a corrugated iron barn, on the left. Beyond it, is a gap through which we can see a dip, or a 'lag' in the fiels below, near a small, concrete hut. When this area is ploughed, half an acre of burnt stones and charcoal is revealed, evidence of the existence of a Neolithic Fulacht Fia - there are, in fact, two in the field. A watercourse would have passed through this - it is still the natural path for water. A spur, taken off the watercourse, would have been dammed, to form a pool. A large fire was made, and rocks were heated, then dropped into the pool to make the water boil. Food was then cooked in the pool. Judging by the large number of burnt stones, this must have been something of a party venue.

An archaeologist, examining the remains, found the skeleton of a large animal which he hope might be an ancient Irish elk but, sadly, turned out to be a more recently deceased horse.

The owner of the Fulachta Fian land showed me a "bullaun stone" which once stood in the field. It is a block of stone, a metre square, with a bowl-like depression in the middle. The exact function of bullaun stones isn't clear; theories advanced are that they were mortars for grinding grain, fonts associated with early Christian worship, or used in shallow wells with curative powers.

The farmer removed it, and deposited it on a ditch where it is quite safe - if anything safer - deep in the undergrowth. He hopes to restore it to its original position in the field.

Site of a water mill at the head of Whitecastle Creek

(4) After leaving the gap below the tattered corrugated barn, we turn right along the verdant lane, passing a ruined gable of brickwork, to the left, and again turning left at the end. The green road now ends, and we cross in front of the farmyard. A gate ahead exits onto a farm lane which meets a small road. Although our route will be bearing left, a brief diversion to the right, towards the creek, is well worthwhile. Twenty or so yards along, a white gate, with a stone stile beside it, accesses a small country graveyard. The headstones, beautifully lettered, are plain blocks of limestone, most of them well weathered, some going back to the mid 18th century, with a few from recent times. A large sycamore - not a yew - grows at centre. The ground is hillocky. On one side, is the ruins of a small building, now invaded by ivy and brambles, with a heavy stone lintel over what was, perhaps, the fireplace. This was the site of a chapel built by priests who fled England in dissent after the Synod of Whitby, AD. 664, which saw the old Celtic church fall under the sway of the Roman dispensation. It was for their chapel - Tig Sasanach (the Englishmen's house) - that the area was named Tisaxon.

(5) We return to the mouth of the farm lane and follow the narrow road that leads up the hill away from it. The verges and ditches have the typical mix of wildflowers and flowering shrubs, celandine, primroses, Herb Robert, ramsons, dandelions, violets, foxgloves, montbretia, fuschia, blackthorn and whitethorn.

The blackthorn flowers appear on the bare branches of the bushes (known as "sceacs' in West Cork) and the flowers give way to small leaves, amongst which the black sloes grow. These are the original wild plums; although bitter and tart, they have been cultivated to produce one of the sweetest of all fruits, the Victoria plum. Picked after frost, pricked and left to sit for months in a jar with equal amounts of sugar and poteen (Irish 'moonshine'), they make a very potable drop of Christmas spirit.

Following on the blooming blackthorns, the hawthorn or may blossom bears masses of creamy or pinkish flowers. Haws are the fruit, invaluable to birds in winter and attracting redwing and fieldfare thrushes from Russia and Scandinavia after their own crop is exhausted.

Kingfisher perched over the shallows

The over-cutting of hedgerows by local authorities has lately been a vexed issue. The latter two species have suffered more than decimation; instead of glorious white corridors in April and May, our roadsides have looked war zones, with torn limbs, shorn stumps and uprooted trunks. In early 1998, a galloping mania to cut down trees gripped every county council and landowner in Ireland. Outraged articles and letters in the newspapers were, no doubt, instrumental in inspiring a 'revised' county councils' policy. The REPS conservation programme for farmers was also blamed for encouraging over-cutting and it, too, may require revision. Hopefully, in future, hedges will be cut only before the nesting season, and only as much as road safety requires.

(6) A few hundred yards along, we take a right turning, plunging downhill. We shortly see White Castle, a fortified house, in a field on the left. Only a single gable with some battlements remains. It was built by a Norman family, the Roches, prominent local merchants in the 16th century. It looks very stark and alone, standing in the middle of the green field. We pass a well on the right, and a stream running along the roadside, the banks of which are covered in delicate white stitchworth in spring. Then, too, the hillside opposite is blanketed in flowering gorse, fat on the stem like brilliant yellow bottle-brushes. On warm days, the air is heady with its sweet, coconut scent.

Reaching the main road, we see a small bridge, once the site of a water mill. The creek was then wider and deeper, with a quay for the boats that served the mill. The stream flows down from Millwater, the site of the Battle of Kinsale, 1601. Following the Slaughtering at the Ford, an episode in the battle, the creek, like the Erne in the James Clarence Mangan poem, 'My Dark Rosaleen' ran "red with redundance of blood" . In the same poem, Mangan wrote, "And Spanish ale shall give you hope...". In the event, Spanish hope died in Kinsale, and the Irish earls took flight for Europe, never to return (see Brown's Mills Walk).

(7) The inlet here, Whitecastle or Ballinacurra Creek, is tidal up to this point, as evidenced by the seaweeds on the shores. As we turn right and take the road along its western edge, we see that it winds between wooded banks and is almost 'picture postcard' in its beauty. Herons fish beneath the trees, red-shanks and curlew probe the mud banks, mallard and teal dabble in the shallows. Shelduck hoover the mud for small crustaceans, their brilliant dark green, white and chestnut plumage dramatically mirrored in the water. Laurels edge the right side of the road, tall as a house. It is a wide but quiet road, where we rarely encounter much traffic. In the evening stillness, the creek is calm, the surface broken here and there by slow grey mullet feeding on the weed. Big trees line the opposite bank. Peace reigns.

We pass the small road that leads to the graveyard visited earlier. Behind the tall laurels on our right lie the fields of Tisaxon. In April, bluebells, extraordinarily blue, carpet the verge. Walking this lovely creek-side road, we reach, almost too soon, the Bandon River, the bridge, and the corner where we began.